To Martin.
from Barbara
Christmas 1977